The Meaning

THE MEANING OF GIFTS

OF GIFTS

PAUL TOURNIER

Translated by JOHN S. GILMOUR

JOHN KNOX PRESS
RICHMOND, VIRGINIA

Eighth printing 1973

The German original edition was published under the title: *Geschenke und ihr Sinn,* Rascher Verlag, Zürich.

This translation was made from *Des Cadeaux, Pourquoi?,* published in 1961 by Editions Labor et Fides, Geneva.

International Standard Book Number: 0-8042-2124-3
Library of Congress Catalog Card Number: 63-19122
© M. E. Bratcher 1963
Printed in the United States of America

The Meaning of Gifts

FOR A LONG TIME I have wanted to write about gifts. What has been told me in confidence has impressed upon me the importance of their role in life. Gifts have many meanings, deep and subtle, both for those who give and those who receive. The significance is no less for those who hope for, but do not receive; nor is it less for those who do not give or do not receive the gifts proffered to them.

Here I am, on vacation, happy to be able to apply myself to writing. Yet, before giving myself the pleasure of undertaking a new work, I have wanted to finish up other works I have promised. This task is a kind of present which I've given myself and which I enjoy as a reward for finishing off other duties. Thus I find myself deep in this study. There are gifts not only for others; there are those we give ourselves, generous or parsimonious, according to the formation we have had.

There is, as well, a whole series of rewards or punishments which we give ourselves as prizes for our accomplishments. We set them up to benefit ourselves in two ways: both to receive the prize and to fulfill the task. First of all there are those which we allow ourselves in order to put ourselves into a better mood before assuming the less agreeable tasks. Then there are those we promise ourselves afterward, as a reward. And yet, when can we ever feel that we're up-to-date in our several responsibilities? At the very moment these words are being written my wife may well want me to make her the gift of a little time, the very thing which I measure out so sparingly to her when I am weighted down by consultations, lectures, correspondence, and so on.

Yet, my writing is also done for my wife, for she lovingly keeps a collection of all my books and published articles. When I earn some money from them, I always feel as if I were making her a present. It is just as though I did not profit by the money just as much as she, and just as though I were not a more profligate spender. Likewise, my writing is a kind of gift being prepared for the readers both known to me and unknown. When they write and express thanks for something I have written, I am very deeply moved. Thus, it becomes again a gift which I am presenting to myself; it is not just for the pleasure of writing but equally for the public recognition so much coveted by me.

On the other hand, vacation time is for spending, not earning. It is a kind of truce in the midst of life's warfare. It is likewise a gift to which everyone feels he has a legal right, ever since our changing way of life has generalized the two-week holiday. I watch my money less closely than normally; I buy frivolously, things I would never permit myself at any other time. I feel quite free to waste time or to use it, according to my own good pleasure. I do not forget my friends. For them I shall take back a little surprise, or else perhaps simply the gift of thought, transmitted by a postcard.

Good and bad conscience constantly play a part in the number of gifts, pleasures, or self-indulgences which we allow or refuse ourselves. Everyone takes care not to spoil himself, or at the very least, not to let it appear so. A man on vacation, or after passing a test, will allow himself things he would never dare do without such a pretext; a patient similarly will celebrate some minor success by taking chocolate, or wine, or a cigarette, something in which he finds a special satisfaction, all of this quite against doctor's orders. Then there are consolation prizes for disappointments or upsets, and other types of gifts self-given in order to fill the void left when others do not make us gifts. Someone has told me of meeting a friend who pointed to her new purse and exclaimed, "Look at the beautiful gift I received from my husband!" "But I thought you were single!" replied the other. "Is that any reason," came the answer, "just because I am unmarried, that I should receive fewer gifts than a married woman? Each year, both on my birthday and at Christmas, I select something that I will really enjoy, and I call it 'my husband's gift.'"

Besides this, many favors we do others are actually gifts to ourselves, either because of the pleasure that their doing affords us or else because of a pleasure which we would not allow ourselves without such a pretext. Thus a little boy suddenly becomes very co-operative in running errands for his mother, either for the pleasure of riding his new bicycle or of seeing the groceryman's young daughter. Sometimes I, too, will offer to drive someone home just for the pleasure of the drive or of showing him the superiority of my car. From such motivations our scruples, our connivances, and our crazy episodes are spawned innumerable. Someone makes a gesture of great generosity, while in reality he has for a long time been secretly waiting for the chance, for his own satisfaction. Many times, also, people arrange for others to present them with gifts which they would not dare buy for themselves.

Personally, I should like to be always making gifts—to everybody as well as to myself. But, is it really in order to make others happy, or is it in fact for my own satisfaction in making others happy? Is it in order to be appreciated by others? God gives me the gift of 24 hours a day; yet he is kind enough to accept in return the little time I give back to him. Happily he is interested in all that I do and is not selfish. Thus I am able to consider as a gift not only the time I set aside for worship but also the time I spend in all my other activities.

When a father enjoys seeing his child playing with the toys he has given him, is it not the child who is giving to his father, unknowingly, the gift of his joy? But let the child turn from those toys for some given by another person. Then, very clearly, he is withholding that gift from his father.

There are parents who, concerned with their child's education, instead of unnecessary toys, give only "useful gifts." Thus the little girl who was hoping for a bicycle discovers that she is given a dress. She knows very well that her parents would have had to buy her a dress, birthday or no birthday. Yes, they've chosen a more luxurious dress, but is it not for their own vanity? What they call a beautiful dress is one that they, not their daughter, find beautiful. She may well envy the more modest dress of a friend while her parents choose for her one that looks like the dress that wealthy friends have gotten their daughter.

Thus there are many gifts which really are not gifts. I think of the strict education one woman received in an austere and pious setting. Whenever she had done something particularly well, had worked hard to pick the garden fruit or had tidied up all her room, she was given two pennies as a reward, but with the added remark, "You will give these to the missionary work among the African boys and girls." Her parents might better have given directly to the Mission and have saved their daughter from being repulsed.

All day long I hear tales of lives and many childhood memories. A good part of them is about gifts received and gifts not received, the magical surprises of Christmas, and also its disappointments. Yes, the fairy tale of Christmas! The waiting, the element of surprise, the locked-up cupboard containing the gifts, the running and guessing of the imagination, the rituals—stockings hanging on the fireplace, or the poetry that must be recited before the gifts can be opened. For children, as for adults, gift means party and party means gift. And no one can say how great is the thirst for parties and gifts which lies hidden in every human breast, even in the oldster's, who feigns surprise as he exclaims, "But you shouldn't have done it! I'm too old to be receiving gifts!"

The mystery of the surprise plays a big role. Basically, everyone is always living in a vague and more or less conscious hope of someday receiving something for which he had never dared ask, some regal gift symbolized so well in our fairy tales. Doubtless, fairy tales captivate us because of their marvelous poetry. Yet, their power lies also in what Jung has called the "collective unconscious," that which unites all men from one pole to the other, and from the most civilized to the most primitive, that which stirs them all in the presence of archetype-images. They also grip us because of a certain "symbolic accomplishment," as Mme. Séchehaye[1] has called it: Both in the child and in the adult there is identification with the hero to whom the fairy extends, as a gift, a power that extends beyond

[1] M. A. Séchehaye, "La Réalisation Symbolique," *Revue Suisse de la Psychologie et de Psychologie Appliquée,* No. 12 (Bern: Huber, 1947).

the restricted and narrow limits of our human nature. Through this act of identification, we can at least for the moment live this dream-life wherein time, space, poverty, weakness, and disappointment no longer hold us in unbreakable bondage.

This is a double pleasure, for we identify ourselves not only with the hero of the tale but also with the fairy in her joy of doing good. This is what we feel when we offer the unspoiled child a more beautiful gift than he could ever have imagined in his naïvete, one which overwhelms him. Veritable joy of the gods! The joy of taking a child into wonderland, of initiating him to pleasures he does not yet know, to the discovery of the outside world in his first trip, or of nature itself. This is the joy of taking him to the theater with all its magic, or even to a simple merry-go-round under its many-colored lights and lively music.

Thus parents who love their children look forward to Christmas every bit as much as they, or for that matter, any other special occasion for surprising them. They are always a bit afraid lest their gift will not be appreciated enough. They hesitate to make their choice; they look around, talk it over, and try to recall their own childhood memories. They stop and study the store windows filled with toys and they scrutinize the catalogs.

There are Christmases which remain forever engraved on the child's soul, gifts which were perhaps not the most beautiful in the parents' eyes, but which struck the child, as it were, dumb to the point where he dared not even touch the gift! His emotion was too great for him. Yes, and it happens that parents mistake this dumbfoundedness for indifference or even ingratitude.

Then there is the art of wrapping, of choosing the paper and the ribbon. An otherwise magnificent gift may be indifferently received because the parents have economized on the wrapping paper or else have used an old and tied-together bit of string. And there must be no question of the donkey's ears sticking through the paper, nor of the shape of the package betraying what is inside! For what excitement there is in the guessing and in the overwrought curiosity. The package must be felt and turned over, shaken and pressed between the fingers in order to guess what it is. Sometimes the child thinks he has guessed the very gift which he most wanted, but he dares not say it aloud lest he be disappointed in opening it or lest he disappoint his parents by revealing that they have not made the best choice.

Long before Christmas the joy of expectancy has begun. It is unbelievable how much time children can spend just dreaming of gifts they would like. Also, the hesitancy with which they express their wishes. What child has not known the inner difficulty of trying to put down on paper the "list" of desired gifts? First, perhaps, because everyone retains the hope of receiving some fabulous gift, as we have mentioned, something more precious than anything he could ever imagine. Even the child who knows very clearly what he wants still expects, more or less secretly to himself, some extraordinary surprise.

Of course, there are other reasons. Hesitancy to ask for something can be so strong in some children, and even in adults, that they are absolutely incapable of expressing their desires. They cannot enjoy a gift unless it is spontaneously offered to them. And even when this happens, they may be stirred to such a degree that they cannot freely express their joy. Writing out a "list" means revealing one's secrets, exposing one's tastes which may not be understood, or may even be ridiculed. Or again, is not the desired gift too expensive? All parents, especially the well-off, try to hide from their children their financial situation. Some of them think they enhance the child's pleasure by always telling him that the gift being offered has cost them a great deal of money!

Yet there is an even more subtle reason: to the young child

his parents are clothed in a magical aura; magicians, like fairies, must know the secret desires of the heart and have no need of hearing them formulated. If parents ask for a list, does this then mean that they have lost their magical powers? Or that gifts are no more to them than a dry formality, which no longer deserve the recourse to their magic powers of divination?

Just as the "list" can, then, be justified for the realistic teen-ager or for the adult who knows very well what he wants —he may even prefer to receive money so as to make the purchase himself to satisfy his own tastes—so it is harmful while the young child is still living in the "age of magic." And yet whoever completely grows beyond that magical age? In it we behold the arising of a feeling particular to our human nature: We would rather have our desires divined than to see them carried out by our ordering. As a matter of fact, does not the young man, deeply in love with his fiancée, find the very gift which she has secretly been wanting?

Thus it is always a proof of love that children, like adults, look for in their gifts. In this respect children are far more knowing than we imagine; they can sense very well whether or not a gift has been chosen out of love. A father who loves

mechanics may have had to enter banking instead of becoming an engineer. Yet he still dreams of fulfilling that secret desire, vicariously, through his son's career. So he buys him an electric train or a Meccano set, even though the boy is only three or four years old. Naturally the child walks on it, is scolded, hit, and punished . . . ordered not to go near the set. When he gets great pleasure from rattling noisily a big piece of paper, it is taken away and ripped up. Meanwhile, his father spends hours putting up intricate Meccano constructions and nags his boy for not taking note of it.

In the choice of a gift it is quickly noticeable whether the giver has projected his own tastes into it or whether he has sought to please the preferences of the receiver. I knew one couple where the husband, a great smoker, had built up quite a collection of pipes. Each birthday of his wife, he would offer her a new and original pipe "to enrich the collection," even though she never smoked! Then one day I saw that woman, beaming as never before. "Just imagine," she said, "I just had my birthday and my husband brought me a bottle of perfume. I don't know what has come over him!" I can think also of another who inevitably would give his wife a book, and quite naïvely add, "Pass it back to me when you've read it; I've wanted to read that book for a long time."

Children's tastes can be altogether different from their parents: This their parents often find very hard to accept or to admit. Precisely because they cherish their children, they think the latter should like the things they like; hence they ascribe their own interests to their offspring and reveal it by the gifts they choose. However, the true meaning of love is understanding the other, attempting to know him and to recognize him . . . even if he be one's own child . . . as a person. That is to say, seeing him as a being distinct from all others, including his own parents. The child needs to feel that his own particular identity is respected; otherwise either he will withdraw and become a stranger to his own parents or else he will cease to recognize his personal tastes and will remain a dependent child. In this way parents who wanted a girl have, through their gifts, made sissies out of their boy by giving him dolls or similar gifts. Other parents have masculinized their daughters by giving them boys' toys.

There's a gift for every age. Children, therefore, when they have grown up, quickly realize if their parents accept them, or if they still dream of keeping them in childhood, all for their own pleasure. Each coveted gift is like a forward step in life, to the child. There is the joy of the first watch that "ticks," of the first cigarette lighter, of the first evening gown. In these gifts parents are communicating their whole concept of life, by implication, far more surely than by any speeches. The evening gown declares, "You have the right to dance, to enter into society, to enjoy worldly pleasures in this way." To refuse them is to say, "Keep from frivolous pleasures, keep from love and from boys; you could go wrong!"

Thus there are countless gifts by which parents indirectly give lessons to their children—an alarm clock to teach them to get up on time, a toy stove with which to be amused instead of bothering mother when she is cooking on the real stove, a blackboard to help with the arithmetic, or a trip to Germany to help the child learn German. This is equally true of many gifts exchanged among adults. A pious woman, the very picture of health and self-satisfaction, offers one of my books to her poor crushed husband, and pointedly says, "Here, read this; you'll understand how, if you had a little more faith, you wouldn't be sick so much of the time."

Many parents maintain a jealous control on the gifts presented to their children by other people. They suggest to the grandparents, aunts and uncles, the gifts they themselves want their children to have, and they quite gratuitously specify the article, color, price, and store where it can be bought. They calculate the value of the ones which they hadn't picked out according to their own adult set of values, and they consider that a certain uncle, rich and unmarried, could well have offered something more expensive. Thus, in some families, at the same time as children burst forth their surprise, quite an exchange is going on between parents. Mother compares the gifts her children have received with those of other children and feels deep resentment. There is also at times an inflating of gifts: gifts to dazzle, gifts far more to flatter the pride of the giver than to bring happiness to the child.

For the adult the expensive gift is the proof of deep love. But the child judges from a completely different point of view. The cost of a gift hardly counts for anything. Love's proof, for him, is intuitively perceived in the inspiration which has guided the giver, in the proof of ingenious and imaginative forethought, in the pleasure which he obviously must have had in seeking out such a judicious choice. Very quickly does the child notice an aunt or uncle whose gifts are always marked by a surprising originality and distinguish themselves from the dull, monotonous, conventional gifts of his other relatives.

Sometimes the father and the mother become very irritated by an uncle whose bringing of the gift is a lesson, not for the child, but for them. He brings his nephew the long-wished-for object which the parents definitely did not want him to have, because of some ulterior motive of educational or moralistic character. It may be a drum, to break the stifling silence inflicted by the selfish parents who do not want to be worn out by children's noises. It may be a necklace of false pearls for the niece, which may give her a taste for the flashy, for the dressy, for dangerous pleasures. The child quickly learns how to play his game on such a family chessboard; he knows whom to approach for what, the person from whom he may obtain this or that. We would be unjust to hold this sort of diplomacy against him, for it is the adults who have taught it to him.

Parental censure of gifts according to their own tastes and prejudices may be so strict that the uncles and aunts judge it wise not to risk encountering it. Instead, they make a gift of money, in a beautifully written envelope marked, "To buy what you want." Often the child knows well what he would like to buy with this money, but he dares not say so, for he is sure to be refused, and what is more, to be scolded for such a desire. And his little friend who dared to offer a gift highly disapproved by them will fall into disgrace, unless the child is prudent enough to hide the questionable gift.

Parental preferences for one or another of their children are also expressed in gifts. One girl may well know that she will never receive the pretty jacket which is given to her sister.

Some children never get new clothes. They have to wear out the older ones' clothes when the latter have received new ones, while for the younger children it is again necessary to buy new clothes. At times, however, parents justify the differences by saying that good children deserve fine clothes. A terrible vicious circle is established for all concerned: The less-favored child reacts in jealousy and aggressiveness, for which he is scolded and which is in turn aggravated by the punishment of withholding other favors.

Just the other day a woman told me very emotionally of her childhood memories. One day an aunt had come with a beautiful doll for her older sister. But to her the aunt said, "You don't deserve anything, because you're very difficult to get along with." Of course, the older girl had been jealous of the other's birth which dethroned her from being the baby of the house, as is often the case. But she was able to master herself and dissimulate her real feelings. She picked on her younger sister, but secretly. Before her parents' eyes she was a little saint. Naturally, she became ever "better" under the flattering praise and rewards showered on her, and she was pointed out to her sister as an example. The younger sister became more and more difficult to handle.

It must be remembered that children often are mistaken

and believe themselves to be less loved than their brothers or sisters. They are convinced that the others' gifts are more beautiful than their own. Generally, however, there is no smoke without fire, and a child can perceive intuitively if his parents have a certain preference for one of their children, even though they try most carefully to hide it, to cover it in magnificent if poorly-chosen gifts.

Toys are not the sole proof of love. The time that a mother, or even more so a father, gives to his children, or one of them, just the two—the walk he takes with him, the explanations he gives on nature, on his own life, his confidences—these are priceless gifts whose memory forever remains engraved as the most beautiful of all one's childhood. On the condition, of course, that the walk be not too pedagogical and not too full of continuous corrections: Stand up straight! Don't walk over there; you'll get dirty and rip your clothes! Speak correctly; you make far too many errors in English!

The good-night kiss is the most vital gift, provided it is not used as a reward which the child has to earn by good behavior, or even made subject to humble excuses for some folly committed during the day. Here we touch a subtle and all-important problem: To the child the conditional gift signifies a conditional love. Just as it is right and stimulating to the child

to reward him for some particular achievement with an unexpected gift, it is equally dangerous to use the perspective
of a gift as a lever, a means of obtaining his obedience. For
then the gift as a sign of love appears to him to be a sign of
love which he must earn, not to say buy.

Too many parents turn to this pedagogical area without real-
izing how they are giving in to a kind of extortion, which will
undermine their whole affective relation with the child. "If
you succeed better in your Latin, you will get a bicycle." There
is no relationship between bicycles and Latin. The parents are
happy to give one to their child. But they want to kill two
birds with one stone; they want to taste the joys both of giving
the bicycle and of the child's progress in school. The child,
however, does not so understand it, and he resents the conditional gift because it means a conditional love: "I love you if
you are good, if you work hard, and if you are obedient." Such
a child does not really feel loved.

This doubt of his parents' love will certainly not stimulate
his study of Latin. Rather, it will undermine his work, for at
his age the purpose of work has not yet been understood. He
will only be able to apply himself if he is sure of his parents'
love. Later on, when adolescence begins with its rebellion
against parental authority, this bargaining of gifts for conces-

sions will be able to degenerate in atrocious fashion. To save their grip, the parents will use even more often this sole remaining defense that they have, their power to withhold money, or a trip, a party, even a useful instrument such as a typewriter or necessary equipment for a healthy sport such as skiing, all in order to tear from their cheeky teen-ager a last surrender.

They, too, are begging for submission as a gift from the child. Refusal for refusal, punishment for punishment, the chasm between them will ever deepen. It had begun almost unnoticed, when the child seemed so good-mannered that it was considered hardly necessary to say a thank-you. In many other families, though the breakdown fails to grow to such tragic proportions, nevertheless the element of bargaining and extortion colors all their relations.

I shall never forget what one of our sons said when he came back from a vacation of skiing. It was during the war when fuel shortages forced the schools to close up for one month during winter, which fortunately set the children free to strengthen themselves in the sunshine and on the mountainside. On the day he came home, our child committed some foolish act, which I've long forgotten. I scolded him heatedly, "Is this the way you thank me for the great pleasure I've just given you?" He stood up, looked straight at me, and replied, "Certainly our stay in the mountains was great fun, but it was for your own enjoyment that you took me along. I don't owe you anything for that." I was forced to admit to him that he was right.

It is very obvious that parents hunger for gifts every bit as much as do children. All those cares, all those kindnesses, all those enjoyable times given to their children are gifts which they instinctively are giving themselves. Yet they would receive an additional gift, that of their children's gratitude and submission. But children find it natural to be given everything by their parents. Parents have even gone so far as to list, like so many grievances, all that they have spent in order to take care of their children in their sickness or for their studies.

This is often precisely for those studies which parents, out of their own ambition, have more or less forced them to undertake. This we see in certain adolescents who seem suddenly struck, unable to work or face the prospect of the exam. Such a student always blames himself bitterly for his sudden and mysterious paralysis, "I simply have to pass my examinations . . . when I just think of all that my parents have sacrificed for my studies." He repeats thus what he has ceaselessly been told. In fact, however, his unconscious rebels at this role of race horse that his parents have forced him into. The serious divorce between the lying conscious and the truthful unconscious is at the very root of the neurosis. Other children, healthier, dare shout back at their parents, "After all, you didn't need to have me in the first place, if you didn't want to spend so much money on me!"

Many show no affection for their children except in this indirect way of spending money on them. What children need is tenderness! How often have I heard a patient say, "I received everything I needed from my parents: food, clothes, training, education, and gifts of all kinds, but I never got the love and caressing I wanted so much. I'd have given it all just for that!" Sometimes such a person tells of the impression made upon him, when he was still very young, while visiting in a friend's home. The mother's tone of voice as she spoke to her son, tone filled with natural sweetness, was to him as an unbelievable revelation.

This child's parents had perhaps themselves suffered from affective starvation in their childhood. Because of it, they withdrew into themselves and became, in turn, incapable of showing warm affection to their child. We cannot give that which we have not received. This is a tragic chain of cause and effect which I see in other areas. One man, who suffered a great deal because of his authoritarian and over-strict father who never gave him the gift of an unexpected pleasure or an exceptional favor, becomes in turn a tyrannical father, unyielding toward his children.

One can also dominate others through gifts. Herein lies another chapter of their multiple meanings. When we present an unexpected gift, we have already gained a feeling of power which is delicious to our taste as we hear the exclamations, "Oh! You shouldn't have done it! Is it really for me?" A beautiful gift enhances the one who gives. It can enhance also the recipient, but the temptation to dominate is strong: The gift which is too wonderful does not honor the one who receives; it humiliates him. One which goes beyond ordinary social conventions gives us quickly the feeling of being trapped, of becoming obligated to the giver, especially if we have no means of doing the same for him. In short, it alienates us. Generally, the people who enjoy most distributing gifts generously about are the very people who shy away most from accepting gifts. They are adamant on paying precisely their share of a shared trip, adding often, "Good accounts make for good friends."

This explains why popular movements for reform, which demand rights and not charity, rise up against "paternalism" which the old and good-natured industrialist finds most perplexing. He thought he had been motivated by pure generosity, with no ulterior motive. However, as we see in the reaction of underdeveloped nations when the great powers offer them aid, the recipients quickly suspect that the ulterior motive of domination is present. In the same fashion, young couples often vigorously avoid a too-insistent financial help from the parents, even though their budgeting may be very difficult. They are simply defending their liberty, their autonomy: "He who pays the piper calls the tune!"

The older parents are quite surprised. Few things hurt more than to have one's gift refused. But they are often unaware of their need to dominate which is hidden in their pleasure of giving. We see this at times in a student who, for example, suddenly gives up his brilliant studies to his parents' horror. He can no longer put up with being dependent upon his parents, and his studies would only perpetuate this situation. He wants to earn his own way and to feel autonomous. Often, of course, students take on work, in addition to their studies, in order to gain enough to be independent of their parents when it comes to personal expenses.

Pocket money given by parents to their children is a powerful means of domination and control. That it is too stringently given by some, while others give it too generously, does not change anything. What really counts is the assumed right to demand an account for each personal expense and to maintain the upper hand that money confers. Many parents do not realize this. They even believe they are acting only for their child's good as they hang on to this power; they want to maintain their monopoly of favors, sometimes to the point of being able to choose their children's friends, husbands or wives.

However, among many young people today, as among the nations which are gaining their independence, we find a strange and subtle mixture of touchiness and grievances, pride and solicitation of aid. They strongly react against the middle-class family tradition symbolized by paternalistic gifts; they react against the cult of work which has been piously taught them. They don't want to work anymore; they want to enjoy life, they whose parents were not able to enjoy life. They listen to records, ride around in cars, live the social life . . . no longer in middle-class cafes, but in "joints" where they play slot-machines between their soft drinks. They refuse to wear the clothes their parents would choose and which no longer conform to the style of the day. They show only contempt for money, the commodity their parents worshiped. Yet they need it just the same, because the possession of a powerful, silent-running and very striking automobile, the greatest of all middle-class symbols, remains their first and foremost aim. And it is the parents who must pay.

We need to understand this young generation which typifies our era of transition in which the heartless Marxist or Existentialist analyses have deflated so many ideals without replacing them; or else they offered others equally weak. And then, there is all our modern technical development: radio, recorded music, television, and refrigerator. For us it was a passionate adventure of invention; to them, who receive it all ready-made when they are still in the crib, it is like a too-easy gift—demoralizing. These wonders of our age were for us grown-up children so many gigantic and marvelous toys; to the younger generation they look like no more than colorless tinsel put around life. Youth would deny that which it already cannot do without. But let us not be mistaken, this generation basically is seeking a gift which ours has not been able to provide: a valid purpose for life.

These young people are profoundly unhappy because they have lost a sense of gratitude. They can speak only of rights. Health is a right and sickness a frustration of this right. Healing, so quick now thanks to our antibiotics, is no longer a gift from God. Happiness is a right. Since no one achieves it, despite all our modern conveniences, everyone is the victim of a frustration complex. No gift can bring joy to the one who has a right to everything. Even love has been devalued; it is but a commonplace convenience which the sexes render one another, without there being any deep self-commitment. There is no real giving of the self!

No giving. This word "giving" brings to mind the subtle transition from gift to trade. For it seems to me that it is in this profound human need to give that we need to seek for the desire for trade, commerce, and even for farming and industry. For these "offer" men the goods which they need. That the pleasure of giving is reciprocal, that it is organized into exchange systems, that the invention of money has generalized it on a world-wide level has in no way changed its psychological meaning. The best businessmen, those who illustrate most truly the business mind, are men who like to give, who like to please the customer. They always feel as if they were bestowing a gift with their merchandise, adding again a kind word and a beautiful smile. They also feel that they are recipients of a gift when people pay them.

Effective advertising has its roots in just such an attitude of mind. Because these men are themselves convinced that they are offering what the client needs, they are able to persuade him that it is so. Zealously they add premiums, discounts, and gifts for the children. Yes, men have an avid thirst for gifts. It is very evident in their great rush to clearance sales and bargain days, and equally so in their pleasure in purchasing some object which they really do not need, but which they've purchased simply because it cost "practically nothing." Again we see the thirst for gifts in their desire for "favors," free tickets, special privileges thanks to a friend, and every other kind of gate-crashing. Is it not interesting to look upon the whole of economic life from this point of view? Not just as an instinctual need to procure for oneself the means of subsistence, but equally as a universal, spiritual need for exchanging with others: In other words, to see it as the need for interpersonal contact!

Nevertheless, the over-attractive bargains and the too-sensational premiums stir up the very same distrust which was pointed out in connection with those gifts which are used in order to gain domination. Frequently there is that same fearful attitude, suspicious of some trap hidden behind every generous offer. We recall those beautiful lines of Virgil, where the Trojans remain perplexed before the treacherous horse which the Greeks have left on the seashore. Under its pious appearance of an offering made to Pallas, to appease his wrath, they have hidden an army in its bosom. Then the flamboyant Laocoon cries out, "Trojans, do not trust this giant offering, whatever it may be; I fear the Greeks, even in their piety!"[2] Indeed, there are many poisoned offerings in this world.

What really baffles us is that the most distrustful people, who have turned away from really advantageous offers, allow themselves suddenly and stupidly to be taken in by some crude swindler who knows how to tackle them. People like the Trojans, who wouldn't heed Laocoon but who brought the instrument of war into their own city! To return to the field of business, there are those who mercilessly treat all merchants as thieves. Yet, they do not want to miss out on the special prices offered. They justify their conduct as an act of revenge, to pay back those by whom they have been exploited.

Many other gifts, to some extent consciously, are made in self-interest.

Thus, when husband and wife are in conflict, often we see them go to excess in spoiling the children, at times sharing foolishly-made confidences in order to tie the children to them, all for the purpose of strengthening their side in the marriage

[2]Virgil, *Aeneid,* Book II, V. 48-49.

conflict. It is even worse after the divorce, when the children, who have been awarded to one of the parents, go to visit the other, or the grandparents. It becomes even more complicated with remarriage, when a step-father or mother tries to conquer the child's affection by all sorts of kindnesses. Often the intentions are of the highest, and he is unable to understand why the child holds back in distrust at the proffered marks of attention.

All this is very harmful to children. Those psychologists, teachers, and social workers who work with the children of divorced parents see it every day. It is every bit as tragic when the child gives in, in order to take advantage of the situation and to be thoroughly spoiled, as when he becomes entrapped in an impenetrable distrust. Nor is it any less deadly when, as we sometimes see it, the child is caught between the two reactions, accepting the gifts but blaming himself for his cowardice. No one wants to be bought.

Here I must mention the seeming indifference of so many doctors to the little gifts with which they are deluged by the big drug manufacturers. The latter, of course, are wise enough to present them in artistic or scientific form so as to clear them of all vulgar suspicion. At the very least we readily accept the "medical samples" which serve less as a means of true clinical experimentation than as a means for us, in turn, to give them to those great and appreciative consumers of medicine that are found in neuropaths of every kind. I have already mentioned elsewhere that the offering of a "sample" can serve to ease our bad conscience: Instead of seeking the underlying cause of the trouble and the hunger for remedies, because of our limited time, we practice the shallow medicine of limiting our treatment to the symptoms.

Let us emphasize that at one time not too long ago doctors felt far less like merchants than they now do: They didn't mention money; there were no bank checking accounts; the patient would discreetly slip the doctor's fee in a sealed envelope onto his desk. But now in the age of insurance policies, of the third party that pays, of "payment upon receipt of treatment," this has changed. In the former days, a doctor treated many patients for nothing. Now, he can see no reason for making gifts to insurance firms, those institutions which have brought him under their control. Alas! It was the age of paternalism; we can understand why our present social development was necessary.

Happily, however, it is impossible to price the value of devotion, attention, personal contact, and the sense of responsibility. Patients are very appreciative of these, for example, that such a busy man should sacrifice a little time for them for personal conversation. Strict duty always seems impersonal, the simple fulfillment of a contract. What really touches our clients lies in what we do for them beyond the ordinary. Yet it is all so subtle: Every gift is not useful. It may lift up or it may abase. Our unreserved attention may help the patient to grow, or do the very opposite, to hold back. This is without doubt the reason for Freud's insistence that his pupils charge fees, especially at a time when psychoanalysis was not yet widespread and when the public did not always understand the great responsibility that it put upon the doctor. Quite rightly Freud believed that over-generosity could interfere with the psychotherapeutic relationship of doctor and patient.

It is not just a question of money. Here, for example, is a patient with whom I have always had an excellent relationship. Then suddenly, without our knowing why, we had a most disappointing interview. She left it quite unhappy. Then she wrote to tell me of her reaction. I could only reply that I was as disappointed as she. Then I began to think and try to discover the reason for the letdown. Well, sometime before, I had done a great favor for this patient's advancement in her profession. Was she humiliated in my presence because of this special gift? Or because she could not reciprocate it by showing

greater improvement? Was I expecting a more fervent gratitude in her, greater than her timidity would ever allow? Or rather was there hidden in my unconscious mind the very opposite feeling from the conscious zeal I showed in helping her: impatience, a demand for greater effort, an unsuspected need to extort from her, as payment for my favor, a greater courage in facing her other problems? How often this is true! This is how it appeared to me, and our favorable relationship was re-established when I shared these inner thoughts with her.

I've always had a "soft spot" for patients of modest means, those whom I've been able to treat without charging. No doubt, this is due to my psychological makeup. Often it has been with these patients that I've achieved my most outstanding medical successes. I've been able to give them plenty of my time with no fear of being suspected of material motives. Some of these people have, in fact, succeeded financially in the meantime, but they would not want even then to pay me, preferring to present gifts to me, even as we do among colleagues. It is of course a gift we have made when we can heal a patient, thanks to the knowledge which we have received as a gift. It is just as great a gift that we receive upon their recovery. Our neuropathic clients feel this especially when they are able to throw off the restraints which have been choking their lives. What joy they have in telling us about it! Here, for example, is a client who has suffered from infancy up from a very difficult mother relationship. She has written to me that, after our latest consultations, for the first time she has been able to have a real face to face talk with her mother. What a gift it was for me!

Many clients dream of bringing us news of decisive victories, as a gift in exchange for our efforts spent on them. They tell us their disappointment at not being able to do it. Their disappointment holds back their progress and they fear that we shall lose confidence. Yet, the trust they show us in this way is the finest of gifts, as every doctor is aware. Often, as I accompany a client to the door, I quite spontaneously thank him. He blurts out, "But, doctor, I'm the one who needs to thank you . . . for your time, your attention, and your understanding." Of course, I have given time and attention; but, on the other hand, he has given me far more precious things—a bit of his life, an opening up of his hidden secrets.

Yes, the highest sign of friendship is that of giving another the privilege of sharing your inner thought. It is a personal gift in which there is self-commitment. We see it already in the child, when he has become conscious of his own personality quite apart from that of his parents, and entrusts secrets to a friend which he hides from them. Up until this point his life had been bound up in theirs, his parents, whom he'd never had any choice in having; he has kept no secrets from them. But now he has chosen a friend, one to whom he will now tell things that will not be told to his parents. Thus it is by choosing that the person affirms himself, for the fundamental privilege of personality is that of freely committing oneself.

Parents sense this. They may well become jealous of his little confidant. They may well reproach their boy for not telling them everything, as a good boy really should, so they say. Yet, if he gives in, if he never dares to hold from them certain secrets, he will remain childish, he will not develop into a person in the full sense of that word. He will become a neurotic.

Thus to give is to signify one's self-commitment. This symbolism can be seen as early as in the first presents a boy gives to a girl. Our ways change, of course. In our childhood the inviting of a girl for a cup of coffee in a restaurant was a serious sign; it doesn't mean very much today. Yet, there is still a certain threshold in the scale of gifts: The young man wonders if he is not committing himself too much by offering this gift or that, and the girl if she's not committing herself too much by accepting the gift. The more the gift is unusual, the more it is personal, the greater is the commitment. The greater we love someone, the more we want to make him feel it, and the more we shall be careful to choose him something very personal. We are careful not to give too personal a gift to someone we hardly know. We are satisfied to present something common, our visiting card, so to speak, via a box of chocolates, or a few flowers.

There is a whole gradation from such an anonymous gift right to the very fancy dress which a man may offer to his wife whom he loves. There are a thousand hesitations in choosing the right gift: "Do I dare offer her that?" For, even more than the price, it is this choosing which signifies the personal relationship. The gift which really means something is the one which shows personal relationship, careful choosing; it is the one in which the giver both reveals his innermost tastes and his sensing of the tastes of the one for whom he purchases it. The personal gift is the measuring rod of the friendship, and it is because it expressed this deep relationship that we have such pleasure both in giving and in receiving.

The very opposite of such pleasure is shown by some people's talk of the "burden" of choosing Christmas gifts. This is because here we are dealing with gifts which are required and expected, conventional, impersonal. They could just as well be replaced by a bank note. We don't know what to choose: A too-original gift would be out of place, yet to offer a too-ordinary one would mean the friendship isn't really very important. Generally speaking, those who do not enjoy giving are those who are unsure of themselves. They are always afraid lest their choice will not be appreciated. They are afraid of being reproached for too little originality or else for too great familiarity. Such hesitations turn gift buying into a burden and betray the failure in affirming oneself, the lack of courage in being oneself.

There are others for whom we do not know what to give because we do not really know them, because they hide their real selves, their tastes and interests. They let on that they don't have any, or else that they are disillusioned by life, or again that they have lost any differentiating personal characteristics. Their personal sense of values has been smothered by the conventional prejudices. Such people are extremely hard to please or even to reach. There are also those who have lost all spontaneity, so that we never know whether their display of satisfaction is pretended or real.

The problem of gifts is, in fact, paralleled by the problem of expressing thanks. This is no less fertile of meaning and shades of meaning. Who is there who has never felt badly because of a failure to express his appreciation in full measure? Warm spontaneity is so easily mistaken for affectation! And a perfectly true expression ("I am deeply moved by your gesture") can so soon lose all its meaning. It is even worse when we have to express our thanks in writing, for every phrase that comes to mind seems either too strong or too weak, too complicated or too personal, too affected or too hackneyed.

The more unexpected and personal the gift, the more it touches the heart, but this emotion is not always easily expressed. The more necessary and traditional the saying of a thank-you, the more difficult it is, even when it is sincere. Charity loses its impetus when it is organized and conventional. Just as you give with joy to a cause, a church, or a person, if there is a living relationship between you and that cause or person, in the same way your giving is debased to a burden when it becomes a regular and obligatory deduction from your checking account.

Nevertheless, let us not be too absolute and radical in distinguishing the spontaneous from the habitual gift, as though the personality were implicated in the former but absent from the latter. After all, the concept of personality implies both the affirmation of self, with personal tastes and choices, and also the sense of belonging, that is, the human solidarity which precludes a total individualism. The conventional gift is, of course, a symbol of our human community. This is evident in the ritual character which it always more or less assumes. You meet an old friend, and right away he asks you, "Let's have a cup of coffee somewhere." Don't protest that you have not the time, for it will not only be offending your friend, it will be a display of individualistic violation of the social ritual.

Thus gifts of both kinds correspond to the fundamental polarities implied in our concept of personality. If the gift is personal, it affirms the originality inherent in every man, such that he can never be equated with another man nor absorbed into the mass. If the gift is conventional, on the other hand, it bespeaks the person in his social situation, in relationship with his fellows and not an isolated individual.

Take a look at any social community, for example, soldiers on leave, or a sports club: When they get together it is always, "Whose turn is it to pay?" This is real ritual, real social cement. The same is true of gifts brought by heads-of-state to their hosts, when on official visits. As far back as we can go in history we see such gifts as the ritual symbols of the desire for partnership. The same is true of the family ritual of giving presents: upon engagements and at weddings, at baptisms and at confirmations, at Christmas and at New Year's, at Easter and even on Father's Day and Mother's Day which our businessmen have commercialized so effectively in order to exploit our desire to give.

Certain puritan spirits deplore that our religious festivals are losing their spiritual meaning and are only pretexts for the exchange of gifts. But religion is precisely that which ties men together; it is also that sense of human solidarity which is expressed by our gifts. The rediscovery of childlike freshness is also the rediscovery of the sense of being related to God. It means giving back to the human family its spiritual meaning; it means bringing together human fellowship and fellowship with God, instead of setting them all against the other. Love for God can never be separated from love for one's fellow men.

Let us not underrate the joy of giving or the joy of receiving, for these are indissolubly related, and both symbolize the joy of loving and the joy of being loved. These joys are also indissoluble. From his earliest years, the child shows his joy in giving. He gives what he is able to, a smile, a look, a kiss. As soon as his hand can seize an object, a toy, he holds it out and offers it. Now he may well withhold it from another child, one who would keep it jealously to himself. But he will give most generously to anyone who will get into the game of reciprocal giving. He loves to repeat ad infinitum the alternation of giving and taking back, for in it the joy of exchanging is built up, the very joy which we mentioned with regard to business.

I am not challenging the Freudian theory of greed, which sees it as a blockage in the development of the suckling child at the "imbibing" stage. Certainly the miser shows his arrested expansiveness, closed off from human fellowship. But the infant is far happier than he and much less possessive than the Freudians describe him. The infinite variety of our human nature can never be fully fitted into doctrinal schemata. The infant cries for his bottle, true, but his life cannot be reduced to this single need of his for the bottle. He gives, he loves to give, he enjoys making others happy from his earliest days. This joy in giving develops more and more when the child lives in a harmonious atmosphere. I am in Algiers as I write these lines, having come here to see our grandchildren. The little girl is running back and forth from the house to the terrace from which I am looking out upon this incomparably beautiful day. She is bringing me one by one all the pieces of her doll's dinner-set; how much more pleasurable it is to multiply the presentation of gifts than it is to give them all at once!

For the child neither social convention nor money nor owner-ship count; what does count is the heart-given impetus. He will give all that he finds. It is an act of regal love for him to pick a pretty flower in a public park and offer it to his mother. Why forbid him from doing this? Again, in the game of hide-and-go-seek, which children enjoy so much, they pretend to hide only for the pleasure of giving themselves away again by coming out from their hiding places. The proof is in their happy outbursts accompanying their discovery after such a brief time hiding! The supreme gift is the giving of oneself.

Many of my countrymen still remember my father's beloved verse, the first poem they ever learned and one which they would recite at Christmas, long before they were able to read.

> For the dear Lord, what can I do?
> I am so small, so small!
> This is what my heart does tell:
> I shall love my mother well!
> That I can do, though I am small.[3]

Happy are those who maintain throughout all of life this childlike spontaneity; happy are those who love to stand and look through the gift store's window or drink in the illustrated

[3]Louis Tournier, *Les Enfantines,* Jeheber, 1896. (Translator's version in English above.)

advertisements in the magazines . . . and are inwardly stirred as they think of all the wonderful presents they could give if they had the means! Happy are those nations where the custom of gifts has remained a vital thing, unlike our lands which have been dried up by an industrial and bureaucratic civilization!

This is what strikes us in the East and in Arab lands. When my son was in the hospital in Algiers, after an automobile accident, every one of the Algerians who came to see him brought him a gift. In Greece, we never went anywhere without being welcomed with a cup of Turkish coffee, a bitter orange, preserves, or some other treat. In Crete we visited strangers to us but to whom our Athenian friends had written of us. While in their home, I whispered to my wife, "Look! What a beautiful cup!" Immediately the woman emptied it of the fruit that was in it, and handed it to us, "There! This is for you!" Yes, and she offered the fruit to us, too, as well as some other small gifts.

In 1954 we held the annual international conference on psychotherapy. Most of the delegates were on the huge white boat *The Achilles* as it was leaving the Piraeus. You know how the boat pulls out: We were at the rails following the crew's maneuvers. They pulled up the gangplank, they untied the cables, the little tugboat pulled away at the ship to bring it clear of the pier. At that moment, an official of the Ministry of the Navy came running out along the dock, brandishing a package and shouting at the top of his lungs, "A package for Doctor Tournier!" In our land we would have said, "Sorry, too late! We cannot come back now!" But in Greece time does not count for what it does here. What counts is politeness. So they pulled on the cables, drew the ship up to the dock, and lowered the gangplank; the official lept onto it and ran up with the package. I opened it, and there was a box full of little pocket mirrors, one for the wife of each doctor present at the conference. On the back of each was a view of the Acropolis.

Here we sense what a gift really is, a personal gift. They wanted each of us to return home with a tangible souvenir of those unforgettable days in Athens. As for me, I also had with me a leather briefcase; a knife on which was also a view of the Acropolis, and which was given to me by a colleague, practically a stranger; some candlesticks; a Jewish lamp; a painting given by a group of medical students; a Greek New Testament; and several other objects. As well, I treasure many gifts from Finland and Norway, Italy and Spain, and America—all of them symbolic of priceless friendships.

This year our conference on psychotherapy took place at the

Bossey Ecumenical Institute, here in Switzerland. We set sail this time too, only this time it was on Lake Geneva. We visited Evian, and were conducted by Miss Suzanne Fouché through one of the twenty-one homes she has founded for the rehabilitation of the physically handicapped to gainful work. To us as doctors who treat patients as persons, how could these handicapped people be "cases" for us, rather than persons whom we were going to visit? How better could we make them feel this than by a gift for each one of them? Some of them were learning precision mechanics; the rest were studying accounting. We chose for them, therefore, little pocket magnifying glasses which are equally useful in handling watch parts and in correcting the writing of numbers in an account book.

No, love is no abstract thing. It needs to be demonstrated, to find expression in gifts, both personal and ritual gifts. Many people look down upon our common traditions, politeness, gallantry, things which they call hollow and formalistic make-believe. But let no one fool you: There is deep meaning in such customs. They are intended to please, and in pleasing others to afford a real pleasure in living to the person who is acting.

When a man falls in love, he almost instinctively seeks to present a gift. Even the gift of tenderness, kisses, and time which he spends without measure. Every beautiful thing he finds he feels the need of offering to her, and without hesitation: He knows that she, too, will find it beautiful, for every gift affords infinite pleasure when we are in love.

Yet there are men who used to smother their sweethearts with gifts, but once they were married they hardly ever offered any except on anniversaries and birthdays and Christmases. This is indicative of a love which has not ripened very much, for their gifts to their fiancées were basically quite selfish. They were intended more to assure her as their prize than to make her happy. Now that the prize has been won, such husbands no longer think very much about gifts. Now when the desire to give grows cool, it is a sign of the drying up of affection. Yet, the heart can always blossom forth again, and a wife can be suddenly overwhelmed by the wonderful gesture of her husband's giving his arm to her in the street, even though for years he has ceased to do so. That husband may be quite surprised to find his wife in very good mood for several days, whereas for years he has known her only as filled with bitterness, critical and easily irritated.

The presence of the loved one is also a gift. Here is a woman who dreamed of losing a ring and not being able to find it. I asked her, "Who gave you the ring?" "Oh . . . it was my husband . . . when we were engaged . . ." "So you no longer love your husband?" "Worse than that, I cannot stand him near me." In the same way, when lovers break their engagement, we see them demanding from each other all the gifts they've exchanged. They cannot endure there being any material souvenir in either's possession of their shipwrecked love.

During short-lived conflicts, couples can hide their feelings even from themselves, out of kindness or out of pride. But their reaction to an offered gift may well betray their secret feelings. One of Freud's confidences is very eloquent in this regard. He showed us the tremendous significance of the things we forget. To prove his point he tells of how one day he misplaced a present which his wife had just given him. At the time they were "on the outs." He found the gift again, immediately upon the reblossoming of their love in reconciliation.

Gifts may also be used as a sort of cover-up for a bad conscience. A woman came to see me about her marriage difficulties. I said, "You mean to say that your husband has been deceiving you?" "Yes, I have every reason to believe so," she replied, "for lately he has been bringing me many gifts. This has always been his way when there was something for which he needed to be forgiven." Thus it is that some men always take a little gift to their legitimate wife each time they offer a sumptuous one to their mistress. The gift in this case takes on the nature of a "sin-offering."

The same defense mechanism is found in many other less serious situations: husbands, for example, who bring little gifts to their wife to win forgiveness for having spent so little time with her, their being so taken up with their work, their social life, and their little pastimes. Or again, they may offer a consolation gift for not being able to take her along with them on a trip.

Thus, sometimes a gift appears to be a sort of tithe upon happiness. It affords a small pleasure to the other one, so that we may in good conscience.enjoy the greater pleasure of which the other is deprived. All of this can be quite unconscious, quite spontaneous. Thus the young fiancée in her exuberant joy may shower all her friends with gifts, half in order to win their forgiveness for having outdistanced them, half from the need to make everyone around her share her happiness, all of it so that she can better enjoy it herself.

Sometimes a similar behavior is not from frankness, but is quite cynical. Such as the case of a man, whose wife had forced him to admit to an adulterous relationship, and who answered her, "You've every reason to close your eyes to it, for if I am happy thereby I am also much kinder to you. But if you try to make me break it off, I guarantee you'll not find your life very sweet." Even where it is not so brutally put, this kind of blackmail is not uncommon—the blackmail of little consolation gifts which the husband outwardly presents as marks of affection, but which are really intended to purchase her collusion.

We should also notice in this behavior that the husband is indirectly confessing his faith in the sacred character of marriage. The little goodwill gift to his wife is not simply the payment for her consent or for permission to be unfaithful; it is also a kind of indemnity, and the payment of indemnity implies the recognition of one's responsibility. The law of indissolubility of marriage is, in fact, no invention of churches or moralists; it is written deep down in the human heart. There is yet another paradoxical proof of this, in those who live as man and wife and nevertheless fear marriage lest they should not prove capable of remaining faithful to their promise.

Despite the libertine ideas which men may proclaim in order to cover up their failings, all have an unerasable intuition of marriage's absolute demands. Even the need to ease their conscience shows this. Ask some engaged couples what they think of fidelity in marriage: There isn't one of them that fails to profess the firmest determination. Ask any person who has let himself become involved in an extramarital affair: He knows very well that he has betrayed himself in deceiving his wife, and if he is sincere he admits it. All men know that the "I do" in marriage is a gift which commits them more than anything else, a gift which must be total, definite, unreserved. Not just is it because of the pledges exchanged, or the solemnity of the religious ceremony; it is inherent in the meaning of sexual union itself. To give one's own body to his sexual partner is to give oneself; it is his personal and unchangeable self-commitment.

In order to arouse the highest possible dedication to a cause, an ideal, a program, or to church or motherland, we use the expression "give yourself body and soul." The total meaning of this is present in such exceptional examples as heroes and martyrs. It is equally present in the fulfillment of married love, for this is the unreserved gift of one total personality to another. When love springs forth it expresses itself first of all in little gifts. But when it grows to fullness between two lovers, they can no longer be satisfied to give each other things; they feel the need to give themselves, and this is a part of the meaning of sexual union. When a child is the fruit of such union, each of the parents sees in it the most wonderful gift that can be offered by the one to the other, the most wonderful gift that can be accepted.

The "I do" is a gift which cannot be taken back. Every married person suffers the moment he senses either in his wife or in his own heart the slightest reticence or holding back from the total union so implicit in the ardor of their first love. There is, therefore, a gradual development from the humblest gift right on up to the supreme gift of marital commitment or to the hero's self-sacrifice. This is what the meaning of gifts among mankind reveals to us: Men need to give because they need to give themselves, and all their gifts are signs of that deep-seated and universal desire to give oneself. To live is to commit oneself.

Let us not deceive ourselves: This great hunger for gifts is not so much a hunger for pleasure as for affection. Man's need to be loved is universal and limitless; it is of the essence of life. Freudians have amply demonstrated this point. Jean-Paul Sartre, in one of his early writings,[4] states that the thing which counts in human psychology is not the facts but the

[4]Jean-Paul Sartre, *Esquisse d'une théorie des Émotions*, Essais Philosophiques No. 838 (Paris: Herman, 1939).

meaning of those facts, that which they mean to the men involved. The meaning of gifts is in the love that they express, the love both given and received. All men have this need to give their affection and to feel that it is appreciated. All are equally seeking proofs of their being loved, and of feeling that those who love them have great pleasure in this. We do not want a totally impersonal love; it would only be a dry and humiliating act of charity. Mutuality is the very law of love: There is no pleasure in loving unless the other enjoys equally his being loved.

Every man needs to feel that someone is really interested in him, his affection, his life, or even in the smallest gift possible. This need is imperative, far more so than most wish to admit. Repeatedly, and in a more or less hidden manner, they are going about begging both for affection and for someone to whom they may, in turn, show affection.

It may make them sick. I have just received a letter from such a woman, who notwithstanding has a very intelligent and affectionate husband. She had written to me about minor ailments and I had replied in a reassuring vein. But now she writes that she has suddenly realized that she wants to be sick, seriously sick, in order to be surrounded by more affection and care.

In some respects the great quest for gifts is a means by which we deceive ourselves, and by our little gifts we numb our longing for the greater ones which escape us. And yet, despite this, the concept of a greater happiness to come, mysterious and yet real and complete, stands out beyond all this race after incomplete and partial gifts and indeed gives it meaning. If each gift is a symbol of love, no matter how small the gift, then surely there must be a love, total and supreme, one that doesn't fail. This is what men intuitively await, and what they are seeking in the smallest gifts received each day. It is as if successive little payments assure us of the final payment-in-full. Sooner or later we realize that all human gifts are relative, limited, and uncertain, even the most beautiful and costly of them. Everything that we receive we can also lose. Men can always deny the love which they have been offering, and as we have seen, their gifts are never completely free of other motives: pride, self-interest, or the desire to dominate. This is why the hunger is not assuaged. There must always be new gifts to complete and confirm those already received. This persisting need is itself a clear indication that its goal is ever toward a final ending after which we all confusedly aspire: We are looking for an absolutely unchanging love, one that nothing can ever change. The universal quest for gifts is nothing other than a seeking after God, by whatever name we may call him. For only the One who has made all things and who owns all things can give them without asking anything in return except our gratitude.

Thus, there comes a day when a man understands that all is of grace, that the whole world is a gift of God, a completely generous gift since no one forced him to it. We see each flower, each drop of water, each minute of our life as a gift of God. He gives them to all, both to those who know him and to those who are ignorant of him. But beyond that, though his gifts are completely disinterested, he is far from disinterested in those who are their recipients; he loves us, each one of us in particular, personally. He gives with joy and he rejoices in our occasions of joy.

I have a friend, a German, who was in a Russian concentration camp at the end of the war. There was in the same camp another prisoner, a young minister who came from the same village and who had been his playmate back in school. Of course they asked many questions of each other. "What has become of you? Are you married?" asked the pastor. "Yes," answered my friend. "Whoever did you marry, then?" "Little

Elsa . . . you remember her—she was in school with us." "Oh! What a beautiful gift God has made you!"

It was this last remark which brought my friend to his conversion. Yes, he had been a nominal Christian, like the rest of us, but he had never known God as a personal God. In a moment, by that remark, he saw that his wife was indeed a gift from God, and that all that he loved and cherished was equally the personal gift of God.

You may remember the magnificent passage in which Axel Munthe[5] asserts that everything which is truly beautiful in this world is free: the song of the birds, the wild flowers, the illuminated canopy of the cloudless night! Everything is of grace. God alone is the One who can give freely. Only from him can we accept all without ever being humiliated.

However, sooner or later even this pantheistic view will no longer suffice us. For in this world there are not only gifts and pleasures. There are sufferings as well, frustrations, failures, and vexations, and we are looking for meaning in them, too. And then there is everything that we would erase from our life, that of which we are ashamed. There is everything we should have liked to do, or ought to have had, and yet which we did not do; there is everything that we've done and which we

[5]Axel Munthe, *Le Livre de San Michele* (Paris: Albin Michel).

neither should have, nor should have wanted, to do. But the game has been played; we cannot begin it all over. Even if we could, it would turn out the same way.

It is then, as we face death itself, that all this world's gifts are but deceit, if there be none of another order, of the order of life itself, a gift to which our human strength cannot attain by itself, despite all its efforts, joys, and triumphs. The great gift, the only one which can be unchanging in value, is the assurance of life beyond the grave, of peace beyond our remorse. It is the assurance of reconciliation with ourselves, with our fellows, and with God, beyond all the conflicts which have accompanied and tarnished the joys of our existence.

The great gift, the unique and living one, is not a thing but a person. It is Jesus Christ himself. In him God has given himself, no longer just things which he creates or has created, but his own person, his own suffering, and his own solitude, given unto death itself. He declared it himself, just before turning to face his cross, "Greater love has no man than this, that a man lay down his life for his friend."[6] This gift of all gifts is the self-commitment of God himself, who carried it through to the bitter end so that we may entrust ourselves to it.

The almost unbelievable news of the revelation is that it

[6]John 15:13, R.S.V.

really is a gift. It is free, without reservation and without recall. Whatever our virtues may be, whatever may be our times
of repentance, they all would be unequal to the payment of
such a treasure. Thus it is that God offers it freely. He is the
One who has paid its price, in the death of his Son. The
erasure of all our failings and all our remorse, of all our regrets
and our rebellion, what a gift it is! The redemption of all our
joys about to be swallowed up in death, and their fulfillment
in eternal joy itself—what a gift indeed!

The gift does not end at death, for Christ went beyond the
cross—he rose from the dead; he is seated on God's right hand;
he shall come. He told us that he will gather men from the
four corners of the earth so that they may partake of his glory
even as he has partaken of their sufferings. Then it is that all
suffering, frustration, and humiliation will have found meaning: participation in the imperishable fellowship of God who
himself has suffered in order to present it to us as a gift.

Should then the little gifts of our daily existence lose their
importance in the face of such a great and unique gift? Many
men have thought so. Once they discovered the riches of
divine love and forgiveness, they turned their eyes away from
this world in order to contemplate nothing but heaven. But
this shows that they had not yet grasped the meaning of the

gospel, for the gospel is never a flight from reality. It is, rather, an act of incarnation in this real world. The same divine love created this world that now saves it from disintegration—the love of Jesus Christ.

Such is the biblical point of view, revealing a God of action, One who enters into human history, who is ceaselessly concerned about our world even in its smallest details, and in every man at every moment of his life. He does not hold anything here below in contempt, for all these are symbolic of the reality above. Before calling the disciples away from their fishing nets, Jesus gave them the finest gift they could have desired, a miraculous catch. Often he brought them back to those shores and spoke with them of the trades of men and of the beauty of nature in order to help them grasp the meaning of life and of the plan of God.

Far from turning us away from the world, Christ directs us to it. He awakens within us an altogether new concern for it. Then, just as little children, we can enjoy all the little gifts of this earthly life, seeing in them so many signs of that great and final gift which awaits us.